EASTER

More Than 50 Years of Celebrating Life's Most Treasured Moments

Vol. 59, No. 1

Sweet spring, full of sweet days and roses, a box where sweets compacted lie.
—George Herbert

IDEALS—Vol. 59, No. 1 January MMII IDEALS (ISSN 0019-137X, USPS 256-240)
is published six times a year: January, March, May, July, September, and November by
IDEALS PUBLICATIONS, a division of Guideposts
39 Seminary Hill Road, Carmel, NY 10512.

Title IDEALS registered U.S. Patent Office. Printed and bound in USA by Quebecor Printing.

Printed on Weyerhaeuser Husky. The paper used in this publication meets the minimum requirements of
American National Standard for Information Sciences—
Permanence of Paper for Printed Library Materials, ANSI Z39.48-1984.

Periodicals postage paid at Carmel, New York, and additional mailing offices.
POSTMASTER: Send address changes to Ideals, 39 Seminary Hill Road, Carmel, NY 10512.
For subscription or customer service questions, contact Ideals Publications,
a division of Guideposts, 39 Seminary Hill Road, Carmel, NY 10512. Fax 845-228-2115.

Reader Preference Service: We occasionally make our mailing lists available to
other companies whose products or services might interest you.
If you prefer not to be included, please write to Ideals Customer Service.

ISBN 0-8249-1171-7 GST 893989236

Visit *Ideals*'s website at www.idealspublications.com

Cover Photo: Dutch crocus. Jane Grushow/Grant Heilman Photography.
Inside Front Cover: Blue Koi. *Mary Kay Krell, Artist.*
Inside Back Cover: Primroses and Bluebells. *Samuel Sidley, Artist. Christie's Images.*

Thou sendest forth thy spirit, they are created:

Awakening

Brian F. King

Green-clad, the fragrant vales of spring
Their gauntlets fling to winter's might,
And winds through waking woodlands sing
Blithe morning songs of sheer delight.
Now gray barns drowse 'neath smiling skies,
Where cloud ships drift their aimless ways,
And dream with vision old and wise
Of blossom-scented summer days.
Now vanquished snows retreat and yield
As spring's bright blossoms take the field.

Edith Shaw Butler

The snowdrop and the crocus pierce the sod.
I hear the voice of gladness on the land;
A bluebird sings a hymn of joy to God.
I feel the pulsing earth beneath my hand.
I see the green of spring come back to hills
Long deep in snow, long deep in frost and snow;
How thus a good Creator yet fulfills
The promises of centuries ago.
"O Lord, how great Thy works," the psalmist sang,
"Praise Him for all the precious things of earth."
For something out of nothing never sprang;
There must be seed before there can be birth.
His ways are goodness, and His thoughts are deep
Who wakes the earth anew from winter sleep.

A hill sports a carpet of bigleaf lupine in California's Redwood National Park. Photo by Terry Donnelly.

and thou renewest the face of the earth.—Psalm 104:30

Melody of Spring

Joyce Inman Moore

I think I may have been in love with spring
Since first we met; still admiration grows
With each returning as I watch her bring
Convincing charm no other season knows.

Her sky is April-blued with magic tone.
And sunlight copper-veils a mighty span
Creating lyric mood that claims my own
To bring about the beauty of her plan;

Till I emerge with an affair of heart
That knows unbounded joy with each new year
For having shared again a special part
Of this recurrent melody I hear.

This page: Kirkwood Gardens in Mansfield, Ohio, offers a seat among the tulips. Photo by William H. Johnson/Johnson's Photography. Overleaf: Keukenhof Gardens, near Lisse, Netherlands, welcomes spring with a wealth of color. Photo by Dianne Dietrich Leis/Dietrich Photography.

The Voice of Spring

Felicia Hemans

I come, I come! Ye have called me long.
I come o'er the mountains with light and song;
Ye may trace my step o'er the wakening earth,
By the winds which tell of the violet's birth,
By the primrose stars in the shadowy grass,
By the green leaves opening as I pass.

I have breathed on the South,
and the chestnut flowers
By thousands have burst from the forest bowers.
And the ancient graves and the fallen fanes
Are veiled with wreaths on Italian plains.
But it is not for me, in my hour of bloom,
To speak of the ruin or the tomb!

I have passed o'er the hills of the stormy North,
And the larch has hung all his tassels forth.
The fisher is out on the sunny sea,
And the reindeer bounds through the pasture free,
And the pine has a fringe of softer green,
And the moss looks bright where my step has been.

I have sent through the wood-paths a gentle sigh
And called out each voice of the deep-blue sky,
From the night-bird's lay through the starry time,
In the groves of the soft Hesperian clime,
To the swan's wild note by the Iceland lakes,
When the dark fir-bough into verdure breaks.

From the streams and founts I have
loosed the chain;
They are sweeping on to the silvery main,
They are flashing down from the mountain brows,
They are flinging spray on the forest boughs,
They are bursting fresh from their sparry caves,
And the earth resounds with the joy of waves.

Come forth, O ye children of gladness, come!
Where the violets lie may now be your home.
Ye of the rose-cheek and dew-bright eye
And the bounding footstep, to meet me fly.
With the lyre, and the wreath, and the joyous lay,
Come forth to the sunshine; I may not stay.

Away from the dwellings of care-worn men,
The waters are sparkling in wood and glen.
Away from the chamber and dusky hearth,
The young leaves are dancing in breezy mirth.
Their light stems thrill to the wildwood strains,
And youth is abroad in my green domains.

A cluster of lily of the valley announces the season. Photo by Superstock.

Swift Loveliness

Betty Fraser

Hold quietly this beauty
And count each daffodil.
Stand still and watch the petals
Unfold upon the hill.

Gaze long upon the greening tree
And scan the bluing sky,
Lest you miss the loveliness
Of springtime passing by.

Jonquil Lore

Jane Merchant

I never saw bright beds of jonquils blooming
In golden hosts beneath new greening trees,
A tapestry of springtime's deftest looming
From all of earth's enchanted gaieties.
But I have seen one jonquil flouting snow,
Lonely and frail and blithely unafraid,
Warming the sun with its exultant glow
Of concentrated courage on parade;
And thus I've learned as much of jonquil lore
As if I'd seen a million blooms or more.

Easter Morn

Ernest Boyle O'Reilly

I rise at dawn and look up to the hills
Where light is turning gray to radiant gold.
Then out-of-doors I see the daffodils,
Those silent trumpets with their challenge bold,
Calling fair spring to speedily advance
With gold-green banners buoyant in the breeze,
Chasing the darkness as a knight with lance
Brought the unmounted foeman to his knees.
Calling the sun to shine, the birds to sing,
The sister flowers to bloom with modest grace,
The lambs to gambol till glad spring shall bring
Sweet newborn light to every smiling place.

Yes, joy is born as light defeats the gloom,
And saved souls sing at Jesus' empty tomb.

A crowd of daffodils borders a rural farm in Clackamas County, Oregon. Photo by Steve Terrill.

Lansing Christman

THE FIRST BLUEBIRD

If winter seems trying in its later days, my impatience ebbs with the swift tide of the newly opened streams and the resurgence of song that comes with the thaw. Little can do more to relax the sharp, taut strings of winter than the melody of the birds and the brooks, floating out through the softening air on a sunny morning.

As I watch the banks of snow begin to soften and note the new spring grayness of the woods brought on by swollen buds, I listen for my favorite complement to these signs of spring—the rich, liquid warble of the first bluebird. As regularly as spring comes, I turn to Henry David Thoreau for his remarks about the bluebird's return: "The bluebird . . . is like a speck of clear blue sky near the end of a storm, reminding us of an ethereal region. . . . His soft warble melts in the ear as the snow is melting in the valleys around. The bluebird comes, and with his warble drills the ice and sets free the rivers and ponds and frozen ground. As the sand flows down the valley a little way, so this little rill of melody flows a short way down the concave of the sky."

The skies are always softer in these days of spring. They ease the chill of the last winter winds, bring out the catkins on the pussy willows in the marsh, and lure the bluebird back from its southern winter, coaxing it once again to accept with man the tenderness of the new year.

The author of three books, Lansing Christman has contributed to Ideals *for almost thirty years. Mr. Christman has also been published in several American, foreign, and braille anthologies. He lives in rural South Carolina.*

A bluebird rests above the dogwood blossoms. Photo by Daniel Dempster.

Spring Equinox

Beatrice Bollinger Lotz

There's sunshine at the window
That bathes my walls in light,
That spills across my winter room,
Paints corners brilliant white,
Brightly splashes snow boots
That by the woodstove dry,
Trails golden streams of April dreams,
Then fades to swiftly die.
Spring sun's a fickle playmate
That loves to hit and run.
But hope, restored, lies waiting
A season just begun.

Gift of Easter

Marjorie Bertram Smith

Now every sound and every scene
Blends with overtones of green—
The mist, the rain, the sense of knowing,
And the root renewed in growing.

With turnings of months,
With circlings of days,
The earth lives again
With flowerings of praise.

Forsythia glows behind a basket of spring bulbs in New Albany, Indiana. Photo by Daniel Dempster.

from HOW FIRM A FOUNDATION

Louise Dickinson Rich

Church activity was not confined to Sunday by any means. There were weekday meetings of the various organizations like the Sewing Circle or Christian Endeavor Society; and every winter there was a big church sale and supper, when everybody pitched in and helped. I don't suppose these were riotous affairs, but they seemed very gala indeed to Alice and me.

In the first place, they were held in the big downstairs Sunday School room, cleared for the occasion of ordered ranks of chairs, and filled at one end with crepe-paper festooned booths. The other end was given over to the long tables on which the supper would be served. Just this simple transformation of the scene of our Sunday travails into a palace of pleasure, so to speak, was enough to make us slightly giddy in itself. Every group within the church was represented at the sale, each within its own field and capacities. The Sewing Circle had a Fancy Work Table, where were sold all the articles both fancy and not so fancy that the ladies had been manufacturing since the fair of the year before: pot holders, mittens, aprons, embroidered guest towels, and nicely dressed dolls. There was a Candy Table, and a Food Table, and a Miscellaneous Table, where were sold all the things that couldn't be classified under any other heading, like a hand-painted plate, or a good, thrifty little white begonia, or a pair of beaded moccasins someone had bought on vacation with this event in mind. Usually there was a Grab Bag, where you paid your nickel and grabbed a wrapped package out of a sack. It might be anything in the world, but chances were that you didn't want it after you got it, because the grabs were ordinarily white elephants, donated by attic-cleaning members of the congregation. . . .

Throughout the year there were occasionally the traditional baked bean, cold ham, and potato salad suppers; but the supper that followed the sale was an all-out effort. Sometimes we had turkey, sometimes we had chicken pie, and once we had roast lamb. In addition there were always, of course, more varieties of jelly, pickles, and relish than you could shake a stick at, hot rolls, and every kind of cake and pie you'd ever heard of and some that you hadn't. You didn't pay by the plate. You paid a flat rate for the supper, and that meant all that you could eat. Seconds on everything were standard, thirds common, and fourths not unknown. The choosing of your pieces of pie and cake was a nerve-racking business. Even the most sanguine couldn't hope to sample them all. The human stomach does have its limits of expansion. But every woman who had been solicited for a dessert had quite naturally put her best foot as far forward as it would go, sparing neither the butter nor the eggs. There was one dark, rich chocolate cake with a thick, buttery mocha frosting—But why torture myself at this late date?

The hot roast lamb supper I remember particularly, since it was the subject of a long and stubborn altercation. Our mother served on the supper committee that year. In fact, she served most years, when the *Independent* would let her, although it was the policy to rotate the work so that the same women didn't do it all. But our parents felt that since they couldn't make as large a cash contribution as many others did and as they would have liked to have done, they should give all the more freely of their time and energies. The church was really the gainer, as our mother was an unusually conscientious, quick, and reliable worker, and her

Dressed in their Sunday best, a group of ladies gather outside following the church supper. Image from Grant Heilman Photography.

services worth more than money.

She'd spend the whole day of the supper at the church and attend all the committee meetings faithfully; and because she didn't have anyone to leave us with and we were too small to be left alone, she took us along with her. We understood that we were to be quiet and good and keep out from under foot; and we obeyed instructions. We found that it paid. End pieces of cake came our way, pieces that were slightly crumbly or unevenly iced; and if the first cutting out of a pie looked ragged, we were apt to get that, too. We fared very well, and we also had the pleasantly important sensation of knowing what went on behind the scenes, of being In The Know. *We* knew—although we wouldn't have breathed it outside for anything, having great senses of honor and pride in being good security risks—that Mrs. Blank's cakes never appeared on the supper tables at all, because she used a vegetable shortening in place of real butter, and the committee ladies wouldn't put the Congregational reputation in jeopardy by serving them to the general public; and that Mrs. Hunt's white walnut cake made only a token appearance, since it was so wonderful that most of it was eaten in the kitchen. We knew a lot that we didn't tell.

Lost Magic

Gladys Damon Higgins

This wooded dell wherein I stand
Was once to me enchanted land.
This winding path my wearied footsteps tread
Was once a highway where my fancy led.

The breeze that sighed in that tall pine
Made all its nameless longings mine;
The thrush that sang in twilight's deep'ning shade
For me all mystic beauty made.

The springtime violet in that sunny glade,
The sun's gold streamers through the autumn's shade,
The moonlight's glisten on the snow fields cold—
Ah! These were all of rapture my small heart could hold!

Oh, that some grace the gift might bring
To live again our childhood's spring!

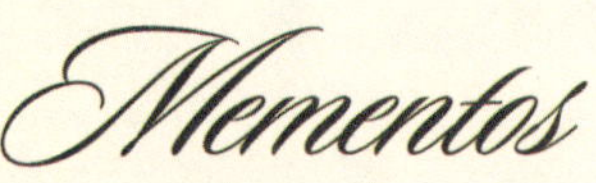

Zelma Bennett

Zephyrs in the lilac,
Murmuring of bees
Hoarding honeyed sweetness
From old memories,
And the gentle fragrance
Of such fragile things
Sparkles reminiscence
Of forgotten springs.

Young friends gather spring's treasure in DAFFODILS *by artist William Gersham Collingwood. Image from Haynes Fine Art Gallery, Broadway, Great Britain. Fine Art Photographic Library, London/Art Resource, New York.*

Arbor Day

Gail Brook Burket

How frail you are. I touch your tender boughs
With careful hand and use the shining spade
To pack moist loam about your sapling bole.
When I am feeble, your full summer shade
Will weave long veils of shadows on the grass.
Long after my last steps have led afar,
I know that people will rejoice to see
Black lace of winter branches drape the star
Beyond this hill which I have called my own.
They will be grateful for a soaring tree
As I have thanked those generous and wise
Who planted trees long years ago for me.

He who plants a tree,
He plants love,
Tents of coolness
spreading out above
Wayfarers he may not live to see.

—Lucy Larcom

A tire swing is shaded with white petals. Photo by Len Villano/Superstock.

A Swing Song

William Allingham

Swing, swing,
Sing, sing,
Here's my **throne**, and I am a **king**!
Swing, sing,
Swing, sing,
Farewell **earth**, for I'm on the **wing**!

Low, high,
Here I fly,
Like a **bird** through sunny **sky**.
Free, free,
Over the lea,
Over the **mountain**, over the **sea**!

Soon, soon,
Afternoon,
Over the **sunset**, over the **moon**;
Far, far,
Over all bar,
Sweeping on from star to **star**!

No, no,
Low, low,
Sweeping **daisies** with my **toe**.
Slow, slow,
To and fro,

Slow—
slow—
slow—
slow.

Two friends share a swinging throne in Reach for the Sky, *an original oil painting by Donald Zolan.*

ZOLAN

Simply Spring

Ann Schneider

Little boy strolling in a shower,
You find such delight
Kicking up the pools of water
With your spirit taking flight
To the crescendo of myriads of raindrops
Beating on your umbrella top
While aimlessly you keep meandering,
Straddling puddles with your hop, hop, hop.
Little boy, you have no worry
Of wet feet, wet socks or shoes,
But find pleasure in springtime showers
In this nonchalant manner you choose.
Your irresistible plight is enchanting
In April's wet springtime air,
Plodding through the rhythmic raindrops
In your carefree solitaire.

One Rainy Day

Marcia Krugh Leaser

Three kids met with a mud hole
One wet and rainy day,
And naturally they had to jump
Right into it and play.

Before their play was over,
They were soaked from sock to soul.
In fact each and every one of them
Was wetter than the hole.

A young boy makes the most of a rainy day. Photo by Jim Cummins/FPG International.

Collector's Corner

Vintage Candy Containers

Laurie Hunter

I would be surprised if my friend Sandra ever offered me a piece of candy straight from the bag. She knows that coffee should be served in a china cup, that it's no more trouble to make your own cookies than it is to buy them, and that candy—to really do it justice—should be presented in its own special container. Sandra predictably keeps her goodies stashed in containers selected just for that purpose. Halloween treats are found in a metal, pumpkin-shaped container she keeps on the top of her refrigerator just out of reach from her many grandchildren. Christmas candies reside in festive fruitcake tins. Foil-wrapped Easter eggs arrive in a hand-painted, ceramic, egg-shaped wheelbarrow pushed by a mischievous-looking bunny. Likewise, everyday lemon drops are kept in a practical glass jar near the napkins, salt, pepper, and other kitchen necessities. At Sandra's house, having to dip your hand into a crinkly plastic bag for a piece of candy would disqualify the sweet from being a treat.

When I first saw Sandra's collection of vintage candy containers, I was delighted to discover that the pieces were much more interesting than the nondescript candy dishes I own. Made of a variety of materials and fashioned into charming and whimsical shapes, the containers in her collection elevate a piece of candy into a prize.

A member of the Candy Container Club of America, Sandra has been collecting candy containers since she was a young child. Her now sizable collection began when Sandra awoke one Easter morning to find candy-filled papier-maché eggs tucked into her Sunday shoes. Every year, the greatly anticipated "surprise" was the same: two colorful papier-maché eggs filled with sugar-dusted bonbons, mallow creams, or wrapped chocolate candies. Then one year, Sandra had to share the holiday with her new baby brother. To compensate for the extra attention her parents fretted she might not be getting, they gave her a dashing glass rabbit, which she found near her egg-filled shoes that morning. With his top hat, suspenders, and hand-painted whiskers, he won her heart immediately. She claims her collection just multiplied like rabbits after that!

Today, many items in Sandra's collection still share a spring theme. Join her for an Easter luncheon and you'll pleasantly discover that, surrounded by platters of favorite luncheon recipes, the center of her dining-room table abounds with antique, candy-filled treasures. Colorful papier-maché eggs, glass hens, tin chicks, and hollow metal ducks are all brimming with mints, candied almonds, and jelly beans. One container sports a guardian rabbit perched on top of a glass dome; inside, mounds of chocolate-covered hazelnuts threaten an avalanche should anyone dare to lift the dome. Another bunny container is fashioned from robin's-egg blue glass that has been stippled to resemble real fur. Strolling down the middle of the table runner is a family of glass rabbits pushing chicks in eggshell carts. Each member of the procession has a hollow interior, with a red, tin closure at the base, in which to hide sugary surprises. Sandra's most valuable piece is a glass swan boat carrying a bunny, chick, and egg and riding on a base of sculpted waves. The entire sculpture opens on a red, tin hinge to reveal candy tucked inside.

Before sampling the luncheon recipes, I stop to carefully admire each candy container and marvel at how Sandra keeps finding new pieces with their own unique stories to tell. Along with treats, each vintage container houses its own memories, traditions, nostalgia, greetings, and childlike wonder. Sandra knows that when you choose a festive candy to share with family and friends, you can't just lay the bag on the table. You simply have to spend a few moments more selecting just the right candy container to hold the treasure.

Sweets for the Sweet

If you would like to collect candy containers, the following information may be helpful.

History

- To attract the attention of youngsters and adults alike, manufacturers began making glass candy containers into shapes in the late nineteenth century. The first was a glass, candy-filled Liberty Bell, introduced in 1876, commemorating our nation's centennial and ringing in a new era of glass candy containers.
- Tens of millions of candy-filled novelties have been made over the years, from ten-cent varieties to rare designs valued at thousands of dollars.
- Candy containers continue to enjoy popularity because their shapes reflect so many varied interests, events, holidays, and eras.

Getting Started

- Any dish or jar can be used to hold candy; but to qualify as a bona fide collectible candy container, look for those especially designed to hold and hide treats.
- Some collectors choose to collect only candy containers that fit a specific theme, such as those that are related to holidays, history, or war, or those that re-create animals or cartoon characters.
- You may want to narrow your collection to containers made of the same material:
    - Metal—such as a whistling pewter bird, circa 1920, which rests on a hollow, glass, candy-filled mound of flowering vines.
    - Papier-maché—such as a mandolin-shaped box made in 1927 and still bearing its thirty-three-cent Sears price tag.
    - Glass—such as an embossed milk-glass Uncle Sam hat distributed during the McKinley-Roosevelt campaign.
    - Cardboard—such as a collection of vegetable-shaped containers from the 1960s used to hold party favors.
- You can locate additions to your collection at the usual sites for vintage items (estate sales, public auctions, antique booths), but candy containers can also be found at antique toy shops and museums since they were often made for and used by children.

These vintage papier-maché eggs have hidden Easter treats for many decades. Photo by Jessie Walker.

What's It Worth?

- It is often difficult to determine a candy container's absolute value, although rarity or age will usually increase its value. A container with its original paint, stickers, or closures will also be worth more than one in merely fair condition.
- Oftentimes, a candy container's value depends on its desirability. Cute animal shapes or cartoon character novelties may bring a higher price than much older pieces simply because they are in greater demand.
- Unique varieties such as hand-painted items and glass containers in hard-to-find colors are thrilling to discover. Be wary, however, of reproductions, which do not increase in value.

The Easter Eggs

Marjorie Holmes

"Well, dear," your husband says heartily, heading for the store, "I suppose I ought to get a few extra dozen eggs."

"Couldn't we skip that part this year?" you plead, remembering previous nights of Easter egg coloring. "Let's settle for the candy kind. That's what they really like best. At least to eat."

"You mean not color any? Why, honey, it wouldn't be Easter unless we did that. I mean—you and I."

You laugh and say, "Okay, I guess it wouldn't." And you remember how your parents used to stay up half the night playing egg artist with watercolors. And the years you two have perched side by side at kitchen counters dipping those pesky white ovals and tracing names and little messages with crayons and exclaiming over each other's cleverness. And how they always smell so good that you invariably peel a couple and eat them with salt and pepper before you go to bed.

And you guess there is something about an egg; an old-fashioned, elementary, hen-laid egg that has something to do with the basic values of Easter. That reflects its true significance far more than baskets and bunnies and jelly beans ever can. Because, no matter how you fancy it up, there is nothing artificial about an egg.

Maybe that's why, even if they don't eat them, children want to touch them and hold them and work with them, and find them in the nests along with everything else on Easter morning. An egg, like the grass and flowers and birds that have suddenly burst into being all about us, is directly related to life and newness. An egg is the very beginning.

Colorful tulips and eggs share a basket in this photo by Dianne Dietrich Leis/Dietrich Photography.

Easter

Mona K. Guldswog

I saw Easter in the eyes of one small child;
    Wonder was there, a breathless moment
    When trust in God shone purely
    As slim white tapers upon an altar of innocence.
I saw Easter in a mother's gentle smile;
    Joy was there, the glory of His resurrection
    Setting hope to sing within her heart,
    An echo to the ringing steeple bells.
I saw Easter in the hands of one old man;
    Faith was there, gnarled and wrinkled,
    Yet they formed a silent prayer,
    To each sacred word a reverent Amen.

May Easter be mirrored across the land,
In countless hearts a holy flame,
Abiding in wonder, joy, and faith,
An alleluia to His name.

Easter Joy

Merle Marquis Frank

Let children's happy voices sing
And glad exultant church bells ring.
Let flowers waft perfume on high
And people's praises rend the sky.
For hope has sprung from empty tomb
Which sealed for sin and death their doom;
And man, estranged from God, restored,
Because He bore our sins, my Lord.
A fruitful life He offered me
When He made death so glorious be.
His love, His work, His power, His way
He gave on Resurrection Day.

Behatted churchgoers stroll home in EASTER SUNDAY *by artist Leo Carty.*

Pamela Kennedy

And very early in the morning the first day of the week, they came unto the sepulchre at the rising of the sun. And they said among themselves, who shall roll us away the stone from the door of the sepulchre? And when they looked, they saw that the stone was rolled away: for it was very great. Mark 16:2–4

WHO WILL MOVE THE STONE?

It was dark as the three women, laden with spices, scurried toward the tomb where they planned to anoint Jesus' body. They had remembered the precious oils and embalming herbs, but they had forgotten until now the huge obstacle that stood in their way: the stone sealing the entrance to the tomb. They were right to be concerned, for the stone was probably solid granite, several feet across and perhaps twelve or more inches thick. It had been rolled down an inclined trench to rest in front of the opening in the rocky wall. The three women could never hope to budge such a barrier. Recognizing this, we wonder what propelled the women on toward the tomb. Why not just give up and go on home? After all, things looked hopeless.

But propelled only by their determination and devotion, the women continued. And when they arrived at the tomb, they must have gasped in amazement because the stone was rolled away! If we read the account in Matthew's gospel, we learn that an angel moved it.

As I read the account of that Resurrection morning, these few sentences catch my attention. Those grieving first-century women were quite remarkable; they kept on going even though things looked impossible. They took one step after another, moving closer to defeat until they made the joyful discovery that their biggest obstacle had been supernaturally moved. At the very place they had anticipated a stone wall, there was an open invitation to victory.

Dear Lord, help me to have the faith of those three women who came to the tomb. Let me continue to do my best and trust You to take care of the rest.

How often are we also tempted to give up because all we see is some distant barrier to success? How can we move if we don't have a house available or if the prices are too high and the choices too limited? How can we possibly meet deadlines at work and demands at home when time is so short? How can we accept a new job opportunity in a different location when we've already made plans to go somewhere else? How can we start on a new health routine when old habits are so firmly entrenched? How can we face the unknown future when we are barely making it through each day now?

The lesson of these few verses jumps off the page. Just keep going. Just keep moving step by step toward the goal, regardless of how impossible it may seem. Then trust God to move the stone. When we are still on the pathway, the task may seem undoable; but as we near our goal, we find that God often surprises us with solutions we never could have imagined. The women thought they would have to remove the stone themselves, but God had already dispatched an angel to do the job. I'm convinced that God is still in the business of helping His children. When we are faced with insurmountable obstacles, it is the time to remember that first Easter morning. Like those three ancient women, we can keep moving along, faithful to do our part and trusting in our heavenly Father to take care of the impossibilities.

A grand rock guards a path in Oregon's Japanese Gardens. Photo by Dianne Dietrich Leis/Dietrich Photography.

Easter

Sister Mary Agnes

No human eye was by
To witness Christ arise,
But I this morning heard
The resurrection of the Word.

It sprang through night, opaque,
A note so pure and clear,
I felt my spirit wake—
It flooded everywhere.

I know what is has been.
There is a vision new—
I see the universe
Divinely bathed in dew.

The Day of Resurrection

John of Damascus

Now let the heavens be joyful,
Let earth her song begin,
Let the round world keep triumph
And all that is therein;
Let all things seen and unseen
Their notes in gladness blend,
For Christ the Lord hath risen,
Our Joy that hath no end!

Left: Azaleas and pines border a pond at Brookgreen Gardens in Murrells Inlet, South Carolina. Photo by William H. Johnson/Johnson's Photography.
Inset: A stem of pink clarkia is dotted with dew in Douglas County, Oregon. Photo by Terry Donnelly.

The Sun Comes Dancing

Elizabeth Coatsworth

On Easter morn,
On Easter morn,
The Sun comes dancing up the sky.

His light leaps up;
It shakes and swings,
Bewildering the dazzled eye.

On Easter morn,
All earth is glad;
The waves rejoice in the bright sea.

Be still and listen
To your heart,
And hear it beating merrily!

Easter Morning

Louise Abney

Pines whose whispers fill the air,
    birches bowed as if in prayer,
Benedictions everywhere
    on Easter morning.
On the mountain's azure crest,
    far above the placid breast
Of the lake are clouds at rest
    on Easter morning.
Butterflies and birds and bees,
    altar-hills and singing trees,
Faith is born of things like these
    on Easter morning.

This chapel, located in California's Yosemite National Park, stands humbly at the base of the mountains. Photo by Superstock.

The Triumphant Entry

And when they came nigh to Jerusalem, unto Bethphage and Bethany, at the mount of Olives, he sendeth forth two of his disciples, And saith unto them, Go your way into the village over against you: and as soon as ye be entered into it, ye shall find a colt tied, whereon never man sat; loose him, and bring him. And if any man say unto you, Why do ye this? say ye that the Lord hath need of him; and straightway he will send him hither.

And they went their way, and found the colt tied by the door without in a place where two ways met; and they loose him. And certain of them that stood there said unto them, What do ye, loosing the colt? And they said unto them even as Jesus had commanded: and they let them go.

And they brought the colt to Jesus, and cast their garments on him; and he sat upon him. And many spread their garments in the way: and others cut down branches off the trees, and strawed them in the way. And they that went before, and they that followed, cried, saying, Hosanna; Blessed is he that cometh in the name of the Lord: Blessed be the kingdom of our father David, that cometh in the name of the Lord: Hosanna in the highest.

And Jesus entered into Jerusalem, and into the temple: and when he had looked round about upon all things, and now the eventide was come, he went out unto Bethany with the twelve.

Mark 11:1–11

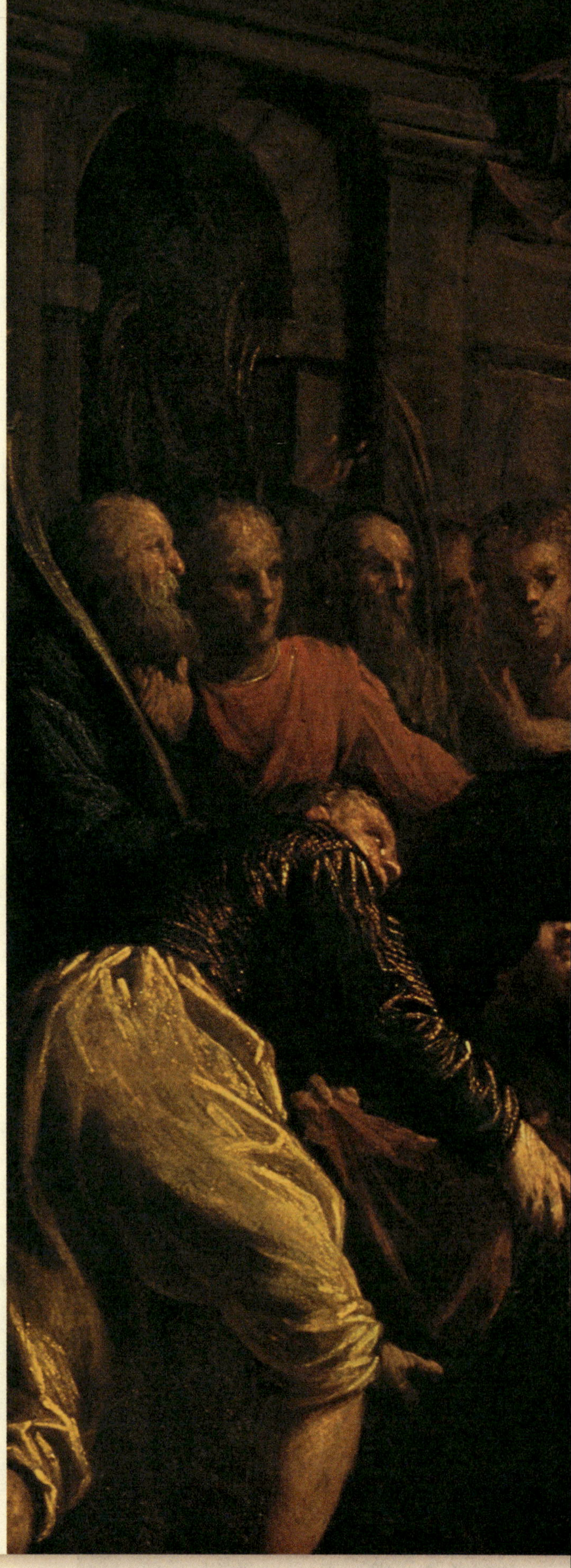

CHRIST ENTERING JERUSALEM *by Jacopo Tintoretto (1518–1594). Image from Superstock.*

The Last Supper

And he sent Peter and John, saying, Go and prepare us the passover, that we may eat. And they said unto him, Where wilt thou that we prepare?

And he said unto them, Behold, when ye are entered into the city, there shall a man meet you, bearing a pitcher of water; follow him into the house where he entereth in. And ye shall say unto the goodman of the house, The Master saith unto thee, Where is the guestchamber, where I shall eat the passover with my disciples? And he shall shew you a large upper room furnished: there make ready.

And they went, and found as he had said unto them: and they made ready the passover. And when the hour was come, he sat down, and the twelve apostles with him.

And he said unto them, With desire I have desired to eat this passover with you before I suffer: For I say unto you, I will not any more eat thereof, until it be fulfilled in the kingdom of God.

And he took the cup, and gave thanks, and said, Take this, and divide it among yourselves: For I say unto you, I will not drink of the fruit of the vine, until the kingdom of God shall come. And he took bread, and gave thanks, and brake it, and gave unto them, saying, This is my body which is given for you: this do in remembrance of me.

Likewise also the cup after supper, saying, This cup is the new testament in my blood, which is shed for you.

Luke 22:8–20

THE LAST SUPPER *by Jacopo Tintoretto (1518–1594). Image from S. Trovaso, Venice, Italy/Cameraphoto/Art Resource, New York.*

The Agony in the Garden

Then cometh Jesus with them unto a place called Gethsemane, and saith unto the disciples, Sit ye here, while I go and pray yonder. And he took with him Peter and the two sons of Zebedee, and began to be sorrowful and very heavy.

Then saith he unto them, My soul is exceeding sorrowful, even unto death: tarry ye here, and watch with me. And he went a little farther, and fell on his face, and prayed, saying, O my Father, if it be possible, let this cup pass from me: nevertheless not as I will, but as thou wilt.

And he cometh unto the disciples, and findeth them asleep, and saith unto Peter, What, could ye not watch with me one hour? Watch and pray, that ye enter not into temptation: the spirit indeed is willing, but the flesh is weak.

He went away again the second time, and prayed, saying, O my Father, if this cup may not pass away from me, except I drink it, thy will be done.

And he came and found them asleep again: for their eyes were heavy. And he left them, and went away again, and prayed the third time, saying the same words.

Then cometh he to his disciples, and saith unto them, Sleep on now, and take your rest: behold, the hour is at hand, and the Son of man is betrayed into the hands of sinners. Rise, let us be going: behold, he is at hand that doth betray me.

Matthew 26:36–46

CHRIST IN THE GARDEN OF GETHSEMANE *by Jacopo Tintoretto (1518–1594). Image from S. Stefano, Venice, Italy/Cameraphoto/Art Resource, New York.*

The Crucifixion

And Pilate answered and said again unto them, What will ye then that I shall do unto him whom ye call the King of the Jews? And they cried out again, Crucify him.

Then Pilate said unto them, Why, what evil hath he done? And they cried out the more exceedingly, Crucify him. And so Pilate, willing to content the people, released Barabbas unto them, and delivered Jesus, when he had scourged him, to be crucified.

And the soldiers led him away into the hall, called Praetorium; and they call together the whole band. And they clothed him with purple, and plaited a crown of thorns, and put it about his head, And began to salute him, Hail, King of the Jews!

And they smote him on the head with a reed, and did spit upon him, and bowing their knees worshipped him. And when they had mocked him, they took off the purple from him, and put his own clothes on him, and led him out to crucify him.

And they compel one Simon a Cyrenian, who passed by, coming out of the country, the father of Alexander and Rufus, to bear his cross.

And they bring him unto the place Golgotha, which is, being interpreted, The place of a skull. And they gave him to drink wine mingled with myrrh: but he received it not.

And when they had crucified him, they parted his garments, casting lots upon them, what every man should take. And it was the third hour, and they crucified him.

Mark 15:12–25

THE TRINITY *by Jacopo Tintoretto (1518–1594). Image from Galleria Sabauda, Turin, Italy/Scala/Art Resource, New York.*

The Resurrection

In the end of the sabbath, as it began to dawn toward the first day of the week, came Mary Magdalene and the other Mary to see the sepulchre.

And, behold, there was a great earthquake: for the angel of the Lord descended from heaven, and came and rolled back the stone from the door, and sat upon it. His countenance was like lightning, and his raiment white as snow: And for fear of him the keepers did shake, and became as dead men.

And the angel answered and said unto the women, Fear not ye: for I know that ye seek Jesus, which was crucified. He is not here: for he is risen, as he said. Come, see the place where the Lord lay. And go quickly, and tell his disciples that he is risen from the dead; and, behold, he goeth before you into Galilee; there shall ye see him: lo, I have told you.

And they departed quickly from the sepulchre with fear and great joy; and did run to bring his disciples word. And as they went to tell his disciples, behold, Jesus met them, saying, All hail. And they came and held him by the feet, and worshipped him. Then said Jesus unto them, Be not afraid: go tell my brethren that they go into Galilee, and there shall they see me.

Matthew 28:1–10

THE RESURRECTION OF CHRIST *by Jacopo Tintoretto (1518–1594). Image from Scuola Grande di S. Rocco, Venice, Italy/Cameraphoto/Art Resource, New York.*

THROUGH MY WINDOW

Pamela Kennedy

Art by Meredith Johnson

THE POWER TO CHANGE

Mara stands just outside the circle of light cast by the fire, watching the men gathered to warm themselves and talk. There is urgency in their conversation. A little while earlier several of the guards of her master, Caiaphas, had burst into the courtyard hauling a prisoner known as Jesus the Nazarene. They were followed by a group of temple leaders who loudly demanded to be taken to the high priest immediately. The religious men disappeared with the prisoner into the inner chambers; but now the guards gather in the courtyard along with some of the other servants, and they sit gossiping by the fire. Another fellow, a stranger, sits among them, silent, watchful, nervous, and Mara focuses her attention upon him. He is large and rugged looking, with rough hands and brown, muscular arms. When he speaks, refusing a drink from the goatskin full of wine, Mara recognizes his accent as Galilean. Suddenly she makes the connection.

"You were with the prisoner. You are one of his followers!" Her voice startles the men, and they stare first at her and then at the stranger sitting among them.

The man looks like an animal trapped in a corner. His dark eyes dart from face to face, and he shakes his head vehemently. "I don't know what you're talking about."

"Yes you do," Mara insists, stepping toward him. "You even sound like the prisoner. Your accent gives you away."

Now they are the center of attention, the slave girl and this rough-looking man from Galilee. She will not be humiliated in front of her fellow servants and the guards. She lifts an accusatory finger and points at him as he stands. "You're as guilty as he is. Why won't you admit it?"

The man stumbles backward from the group; and at that moment, the door from the high priest's chambers bursts open, and two armed men shove the beaten and stumbling Jesus into the courtyard. There is a moment when time seems to stop. The prisoner and the stranger stand staring at one another, and Mara thinks she sees a flash of recognition. Then a rooster somewhere crows twice, rending the pre-dawn stillness. The prisoner turns away; the stranger gasps, then flees from the courtyard as if pursued by demons. Mara hears his anguished cries echoing off the courtyard walls long after he is gone.

It has been almost seven weeks since the arrest and crucifixion of Jesus, the man some called the Christ. Many in Jerusalem have forgotten about Him. There is always some new local celebrity claiming to be the Messiah. Most come and go and no one pays them much attention. Mara keeps to herself, busy with her responsibilities in the house of the high priest. But today is the first day of Pentecost, and she rushes to the marketplace to do her shopping for the household before the sun becomes unbearably hot. The streets teem with visitors from distant countries. Their unfamiliar languages swirl around Mara like dissonant melodies. She loves the marketplace with its myriad scents and sounds, for here she can briefly pretend she is the mistress of her own home, purchasing vegetables and meat to prepare for a husband and children. For a little while she dreams of such contentment, but reality always intrudes. If she doesn't hurry, the high priest's wife will be angry. She turns her attention to a basket of fresh onions.

"Hurry, I tell you, it's a miracle!" A man pushes past Mara, almost knocking her over. She turns to see people from the market dashing along the street, all shouting and talking in a variety of languages.

She grasps the robe of a woman rushing by. "What is it? Where are you going?" The woman stops for a moment and says something about fire and rushing wind and men from Jerusalem speaking in languages they had never learned, giving the people a message from God Himself.

Mara joins the throng and is swept along to an area in front of a two-story house. A man stands, raises his arms, and speaks in a loud voice. "People of Israel, listen! God publicly endorsed Jesus of Nazareth by doing miracles, wonders, and signs, but you, with the help of the Gentiles, nailed Him to a cross and killed Him. Now I stand here declaring that God released Him from the horrors of death and raised Him back to life again."

Mara stares, and her mouth falls open in astonishment. The man speaking is that same one who denied he even knew Jesus and then fled sobbing from the courtyard just a few weeks earlier. Today he stands in the midst of thousands, boldly declaring his belief that Jesus is God's true son! The young woman wonders at the transformation as she stands listening to Peter the fisherman. His words penetrate her heart as nothing ever has. He speaks of hope and forgiveness, of living guided by God's own spirit. It is as if he pours water on the dried and shriveled dreams deep in Mara's heart. She, who has only, always, been a worthless slave, hears that she is precious and worthy of God's love. And she believes it.

She loses track of time and begins to hear a new voice, first from outside, then from within, telling her she can begin life anew. She can be free. She, Mara, is a person of value, not just a possession to be used and cast aside when her master tires of her. When Peter stops speaking, the cries of Mara and the others rise in the dusty afternoon: "What should we do? What should we do?"

"Come," he says. And they follow Peter and are baptized, joining together in a community of believers. Mara still serves, but now from a heart filled with love, as the daughter of a King. Together with thousands who heard Peter's words at Pentecost, she becomes part of a brand new family. It is a family that learns and eats and shares all they have together. It is a family that will change the world because of their Father's love.

Pamela Kennedy is a freelance writer of short stories, articles, essays, and children's books. Wife of a retired naval officer and mother of three children, she has made her home on both U.S. coasts and currently resides in Honolulu, Hawaii.

Emmaus Road

Margaret Rorke

Christ walked with two
Who knew Him well
Along that dusty path.
What He'd been through
He heard them tell:
His death and aftermath.

Confused, bereft,
Bowed down with grief,
Their eyes upon the soil,
What had they left
But mixed belief
In Him they thought was royal?

They argued some
As they conversed
Upon that Easter Day
'Bout Him who'd come
And known man's worst,
But failed to look His way.

Make me wide-eyed
That I may know,
Though heavy be my load,
He's at my side
The while I go
Down my Emmaus Road.

The Road to Emmaus

Methyl Hawkins

Along the dusty road they trod
With stumbling feet and slow,
Burdened beneath the crushing load
The disappointed know.
Their Lord was dead, and shattered lay
Each cherished dream and plan,
Each humble yearning of the heart
That stirs the soul of man.
Then to their side a stranger drew,
"Why are ye sad?" asked He.
"Because our prophet buried lies,
The man from Galilee.
We trusted that His word was true,
Our hopes He did deceive."
And then the stranger murmured low,
"Oh, slow of heart, believe!"
Along the dusty road they trod
With eyes upon the sod,
And quietly beside them walked
The risen Son of God!

A tunnel of oaks lines a road at Afton Villa Gardens in St. Francisville, Louisiana. Photo by Superstock.

Dogwood

Alta McLain

They say the dogwood tree, long years ago,
Stalwart and straight and very tall did grow
Until a cross was borne to Calvary
Made of its wood. The grieving tree
Asked of the Lord with painful, quickened breath
To have no more a part in pain and death.
And so the dogwood tree quite small was made,
A gnarled yet lovely dweller in the shade
Telling Christ's resurrection year by year.
See this! A tiny crown of thorns is here
On petals white which form a gleaming cross.
Here nails have pierced, and blood divine was lost.
The dogwood burdened Him against its will;
But you and I, we crucify Him still.

Flowering Dogwood

Julia Collins Ardayne

The nail-prints still are there upon the edges
Of every petal as the tree still mourns
The Saviour's death. And, lo, within the blossom
The calyx rises to a crown of thorns.
Even in spring's bright hour of opening,
When warm winds bring the fragile buds to flower,
Shaped like a cross the dogwood's snowy petals
Remember when He came to His last hour.
And now abloom in April's nascency
The slender boughs again reach back across
The years to that dark hour on far Golgotha
When a dogwood tree was cut to make His cross.

A nest of tiny eggs nestles among the dogwood branches. Photo by Dianne Dietrich Leis/Dietrich Photography.

PEPPERS
RED

Prayer in a Garden

Viney Wilder

I thank Thee, Lord, that I can see
This proof of immortality;
That I can hear in April rain
The stir of fragile leaves again;

That I can feel the wind that sweeps
Where summer fruit now lightly sleeps
And smell the spring upon my spade
Where warm black earth is freshly laid.

I thank Thee, Lord, that here today
Death's ugly stone is rolled away,
And now beside the empty tomb
I kneel to touch the first frail bloom.

Easter Prayer

Ruth W. Stevens

We thank Thee, God, for spring, when earth turns green
And ice-freed streams play tinkling tunes. The chill
Wind blows no more, so blossoms bud. Between
Sun-stenciled leaves, the first shy warblers trill.

We thank Thee, God, for light and soft warm air;
For daffodils whose golden shine adorns
The tufted grass; for woods where hilltops wear
Blue violets for crowns instead of thorns.

We thank Thee, God, for life. Now spring is here—
Revive in us fresh understanding, give
New wisdom for the tasks ahead, melt fear
With love—You gave Your Son that we might live.

Dear God, as spring and life return again,
Accept the thanks of grateful hearts. Amen.

A raised garden waits to be tended. Photo by Jessie Walker.

Nancy Skarmeas

HARRIET HOSMER

Harriet Hosmer's father wanted a different sort of life for his youngest daughter. He had lost his wife and another daughter to tuberculosis and was determined that he would not lose Harriet in the same way. His remedy was an active, outdoor life for his young girl. Born in 1830, Harriet grew up in the woods and fields surrounding her Watertown, Massachusetts, home. She learned to swim, to ice skate, and to hunt with a bow and arrow and a rifle. She felt at home riding horses, paddling a canoe, and making her way in the woods. She was certainly not confined in the drawing room stitching, playing the piano, and reading, as was the custom for American girls of her day and class. Her father believed outdoor activity would keep Harriet strong, healthy, and safe from the illness that had taken her mother and sister. The neighbors disapproved of this upbringing, and they worried about Harriet's future prospects. But Mr. Hosmer persevered, and Harriet flourished. Her father's prescription for health had an interesting side effect upon his daughter's spirit. While her contemporaries obediently looked forward to fulfilling their quiet and conventional roles in polite society, Harriet Hosmer grew to adulthood believing her future was hers to imagine.

And the future she began to imagine, from the time she was a young teenager, was as an artist, in particular a sculptor. Hosmer loved working with clay in her school's art classes and was pleased with her efforts to make little sculptures of the animals she watched in the woods around her home. Although sculpting is not a controversial career choice for a woman in the twenty-first century, it was considered at worst scandalous and at best laughable in the 1840s when Harriet Hosmer came to adulthood. Women resented her unwillingness to conform to the roles they had accepted; and men, especially male artists, were unwilling to consider the idea of a woman producing serious art.

Harriet Hosmer, however, was not of the sort to be put off by public disapproval. She would become a sculptor, with or without the approval or assistance of the community at large. Failing to find anyone willing to give her instruction beyond her school art classes, Hosmer turned to the one individual who was always on her side, her father, who happily built his daughter a studio at their home. While the neighbors gossiped and one male artist after another dismissed her interest in art, Hosmer continued to sculpt.

Hosmer eventually found a sculptor in Boston willing to accept her as a student. Her technique improved quickly, but she felt the need for more instruction. A sculptor, Hosmer knew, needed a detailed knowledge of the human form. The usual route to this knowledge was medical school classes in anatomy. Hosmer approached local medical schools and asked permission to enroll. She was refused by every school close to her Massachusetts home. Women simply were not welcome in medical schools in the 1840s. But sculpting had developed into a true passion with Hosmer, and she continued her search until a doctor in St. Louis agreed to give her lessons in anatomy. So Hosmer went to Missouri. While there, she not only learned what she needed to learn about anatomy; she also took a riverboat trip down the Mississippi River, where she encountered local Indians and explored the landscape of the American Midwest and South. Harriet Hosmer was now an adult, but she had never outgrown the adventurous spirit fostered in childhood by her father.

Back at work in Watertown, Harriet completed a bust she called *Hesper*. This work won critical acclaim and convinced Harriet Hosmer that it was time to go to Rome, study with the masters, and see the great works of European sculpture. She arrived in Rome in 1852 and studied there at the studio of famed English sculptor John Gibson. In Rome, Hosmer found what she had been seeking ever since she had discovered her talent and passion for sculpting. She became part of an international community of artists, including Elizabeth Barrett Browning, Nathaniel Hawthorne, and Henry James, who had gathered in Rome to seek mutual inspiration. Here Hosmer and other female sculptors were accepted on equal footing; and her work and personality left an impression on all, including Hawthorne, who chose Hosmer as the model for Hilda in his novel *The Marble Faun*.

Even within this community of artists, Harriet Hosmer was known for what public opinion chose to call eccentricities. She wore her hair cropped short, was outspoken and free-spirited, and was as strong willed and independent as her father had taught her to be during the days of her active youth. And just as she had learned then to think little of the disapproval of society, she gave little heed to cultural conventions in Rome. It was sculpting that mattered to Harriet Hosmer, not public opinion about her personality.

Hosmer's friend Elizabeth Barrett Browning wrote, Harriet "lives here all alone, dines and breakfasts at the cafes, exactly as a young man would; she works from six o'clock in the morning till night, as a great artist must." Hosmer wasn't, Barrett Browning would have us know, so eccentric after all; she was merely a gifted and creative artist who lived her life devoted to her work.

Harriet Hosmer sculpted many heroes and heroines of history and literature, from Thomas Hart Benton (the Missouri statesman) to Daphne and Medusa from classical mythology. One of her most admired works is that of Puck from Shakespeare; the piece was purchased by the Prince of Wales (later Edward VII) and later reproduced thirty times due to its popularity. Another of Hosmer's acclaimed pieces, now displayed at New York's Metropolitan Museum of Art, is her bronze cast of the clasped hands of Robert and Elizabeth Barrett Browning. In spite of her reputation as a free spirit, Hosmer's work, most often described as neoclassical, was quite traditional in both style and subject. Her works can be seen today as public monuments, in private collections, and in renowned museums. She became, without a doubt, the foremost woman sculptor of her day, and the passage of years has not diminished her achievement; her sculptures have stood the test of time and are still considered treasures of American art.

It is a blessing to grow up unburdened by the expectations of others; Harriet Hosmer did just that. Every parent would do well to take notice of Harriet's father's gift to her: he taught her to listen to her heart without regard for the opinions of others. As a result, Hosmer did not need to muster any great courage to defy the conventions of her day, she simply did not take notice of them. Because of her father's support and her own iron will, her energies were not to be expended upon the act of defiance, but upon the pursuit of her own dream. Harriet Hosmer became a celebrated sculptor because she was blessed with exceptional artistic talent and because she was confident enough to always hear her own voice through the din of public opinion.

Nancy Skarmeas is a book editor and mother of two young children, who keep her and her husband quite busy at their home in New Hampshire. Her Greek and Irish ancestry has fostered a lifelong interest in research and history.

The Sculptor

Marcia Krugh Leaser

The canvas must be silent
As the artist paints the scene.
The paper too waits anxiously
While the author shares his dream.
The many lines surrender
To the architect's keen plan.
The clay must yield to form and shape
In the gentle potter's hand.
And we, the most unyielding
Of the universal tools,
Must learn to be compliant
In the way we will be used.
God works on us throughout our lives,
For only He's aware
Behind our masks of make-believe
A wounded soul lays bare.

The Miracle of Spring

Ethel Colwell Smith

The miracle of spring may come
To any man on earth,
And tranquil thought may trill with
Life's abundant power and worth.

The sap climbs up. The tallest tip
Awakes in graceful glee,
For April's wholly unconcerned
With laws of gravity.

Fragrant flowers are loveliest
At close of winter storm.
Oh, blessed fact: No fall seed died;
It grew and changed its form.

Then why art thou cast down, O soul,
Why not let hope hold sway?
For crucifixion always ends
In a resurrection day.

The hour is come for thee to live
As the Son of God should live;
To satisfy the Christ within;
To know, and be, and give.

And should some boastful bluster
Corner thee in dusky tomb,
Three days' good work will raise thee up;
Life needs a radiant room.

God's promises are kept, O soul;
Why not look out and sing,
"My God is life, and life is mine,
Sweet certainty of spring."

Spring color surrounds visitors to this bird bath in Woodland, Washington. Photo by Dianne Dietrich Leis/Dietrich Photography.

Brookgreen Gardens

Murrells Inlet, South Carolina

Christine M. Landry

When I was young, my parents would join other members after Sunday services on the church lawn while I often would sneak away to the side of the church to a pathway that meandered through a small garden. At the end of the path, nestled among plants and flowers, was a small bench and a statue of a young girl. I used to sit there and look at the statue and marvel at how a piece of stone could be chiseled into the smooth folds of a dress, the tiny features of a face. Even as a child, I recognized the splendor of enjoying nature and man-made works side by side.

As an adult living in the city, I seldom find time to escape to a garden these days; so I looked forward to a recent visit to South Carolina's Brookgreen Gardens. Situated between Murrells Inlet and Pawleys Island, Brookgreen touts three hundred acres of gardens, sculptures, and ponds. This collaboration of nature and art not only sounded like a happy reminder of my favorite childhood spot, but also the perfect place for a peaceful getaway.

The land that is now Brookgreen Gardens was purchased by Anna Hyatt Huntington and Archer M. Huntington in 1929 as a place to build their winter home. The couple was so captivated by the site, which included such indigenous vegetation as live oaks draped in Spanish moss, that they decided to wed the serene background of the countryside with the artwork of American sculptors and create a unique place where people could enjoy the beauty of art and nature together. Brookgreen Gardens opened to the public in 1932 and now holds the largest collection of American sculptures (more than eight hundred) in the country and includes eighty works by Anna Hyatt Huntington, who became a respected sculptor as well as co-founder of Brookgreen. The gardens are also a work of art, designed in a butterfly pattern by Mrs. Huntington, with the pathways creating the outline of the insect and the plants and ponds decorating its wings.

The sprawling land of Brookgreen Gardens dazzled me upon first view. Carefully designed, the lush grounds are divided into ten distinct garden "rooms," each of which combines plants, pools, and sculptures to create its unique design. The first room I visited was the Diana Pool garden, which was planted with white dogwoods, pale hydrangeas, and white kale. I then strolled through the Dogwood Garden, which combined dogwoods, snapdragons, and four reflective ponds to create its ambience. In Oak Allee, I found perennials weaving through a wall and a statue of Narcissus peering at himself in a pool, all framed by towering live oaks.

I stopped to eat a picnic lunch in the Palmetto Garden. Surrounded by stately palmettos and dotted with African lilies, this garden had a formal feel and boasted a statue of Samson and the Lion at the center of a calm pool. After my lunch, I followed a group of children through a tunnel built of tree branches and trunks until we emerged inside the Garden Room for Children, where we were surrounded by brilliant red hibiscus, orange black-eyed Susans, and hundreds of multi-colored butterflies that flitted from a nearby butterfly house. I watched as the children gazed up at the sunflowers or peered at the sculptures.

My visit to Brookgreen Gardens held many delights. I had not expected each garden room to be so beautiful yet so distinct, and I was amazed at how easily the hundreds of sculptures merged with their natural surroundings. But mostly I was pleased to see children enjoying the gardens as much as the adults. As I recall my garden hideaway as a girl, I'm glad to know that visitors of all ages are still able to appreciate the wonders of both nature and art that Brookgreen Gardens has to share.

An ivy-covered arch frames a view of one of Brookgreen Gardens' sculptures. Photo by William H. Johnson/Johnson's Photography.

The Bloom of the Year

Robert Browning

All the breath and the bloom of the
  year in the bag of one bee:
All the wonder and wealth of the mine in
  the heart of one gem:
In the core of one pearl all the shade and the
  shine of the sea:
Breath and bloom, shade and shine,—wonder,
  wealth, and—how far above them—
    Truth, that's brighter than gem,
    Trust, that's purer than pearl,—
Brightest truth, purest trust in the universe—
  all were for me
    In the kiss of one girl.

And Would You See My Mistress's Face

Thomas Campion

And would you see my mistress's face?
It is a flowery garden place
Where knots of beauties have such grace
That all is work and nowhere space.

It is a sweet delicious morn
Where day is breeding, never born.
It is a meadow yet unshorn
Which thousand flowers do adorn.

A pastel vignette of the season is captured in SPRINGTIME by artist David Woodlock. Image from Fine Art Photographic Library, London/Art Resource, New York.

HANDMADE HEIRLOOM

A decades-old desk receives new life with a bit of trompe l'oeil. Photo by Brent Kane, from the book PAINTED CHAIRS *by Jennifer R. Ferguson and Judith A. Skinner. Reproduced with the permission of Martingale & Company, Woodinville, Washington.*

TROMPE L'OEIL

Lisa Ragan

I do not hail from a family of many riches, but we do have a few pieces of furniture that have been passed down through the years for sentimental reasons. A few years ago I inherited an old student's desk that had belonged to my grandfather. Granted, the piece looked neglected at best, but it was my grandfather's, and I felt an inexplicable desire to take it home. After I carted the desk back to Tennessee, I stored it in the garage until I could decide what to do with it. I considered stripping it and staining it, but I wasn't sure the piece was really worth it. A few months later while I was redecorating my study, I remembered the old desk in the garage and knew the perfect way to bring it back to life: a trompe l'oeil painting technique.

Trompe l'oeil (pronounced, roughly, "tromp loy") is an elegant French phrase with a surprisingly simple meaning: fool the eye. Both professional artists and everyday crafters employ trompe l'oeil techniques to render painted scenes or objects that appear so realistic and three-dimensional as to delude onlookers into thinking they are indeed the real thing. Favorite subjects for trompe l'oeil include architectural details such as columns or pediments, false windows complete with painted curtains, or even painted finishes that look like wood, stone, or marble. For my grandfather's desk, I chose to add a handkerchief, envelopes, and a rose by employing thc tricks of trompe l'oeil. The rose in particular is a tribute to my grandfather, who spent some of his happiest hours tending his rose garden.

As an impromptu trompe l'oeil "artist," I found myself in good company. Examples of trompe l'oeil techniques have been traced back through the centuries to the walls of Egyptian tombs where the story of a man's life was often depicted in life-size paintings. Another early example of trompe l'oeil comes to us in the form of a story passed down from Pliny the Elder of ancient Rome. It seems that two fifth-century B.C. artists, Parrhasius and Zeuxis, were competing with one another to see who could create the most realistic painting. Zeuxis painted a bunch of grapes that appeared so real that birds reportedly flew down to eat them. It is told that Zeuxis then impatiently went to draw back the curtain on Parrhasius' painting, but alas, it was no curtain at all but rather a realistic illusion.

Trompe l'oeil has gone in and out of style through the ages and can be seen in the frescoes of many Roman cathedrals, the painted "domed" ceilings of Baroque palaces, and even Michelangelo's Sistine Chapel. In late nineteenth-century America, the artist William Michael Harnett found himself in trouble with federal treasury agents, who judged his painted renderings of United States currency as worthy of a possible counterfeit charge. Today, a large-scale example of trompe l'oeil can be admired in Frederick, Maryland, where muralist William Cochran painted a plain concrete bridge to look like a hundred-year-old, stone bridge complete with twining ivy. Concerned and unknowingly duped citizens have reportedly called the city to warn them to remove the ivy before it takes over the bridge.

But trompe l'oeil can be enjoyed on a much smaller scale too. Homeowners may include a faux marbled niche in a hallway, a false window in a windowless powder room, or even moss-covered bricks painted on a concrete patio. I once admired a beautiful iguana perched above the kitchen door in a neighbor's home only to be told that the reptile was mere painted illusion. Imagine my surprise!

One of the techniques in obtaining a trompe l'oeil effect is to establish depth and perspective. This means to determine where the imaginary horizon line would be to the viewer's eye. For example, in painting a set of shelves, if the middle shelf is at eye level and is the focal point, then the viewer will see some of the bottom of the top shelf and none of the bottom of the lower shelf. Highlights and shadows also add a crucial touch of three-dimensional realism to trompe l'oeil paintings. For my grandfather's desk, I decided where to place it in my study and determined from what direction the light would strike it, in this case slightly off to the right where the window is. So I placed my highlights on the upper right edges of each painted element and the shadows to the left and slightly lower than each element. This effect helps give the painted images a raised appearance. Contrast serves as another technique that adds the illusion of realism to trompe l'oeil images. This contrast can be achieved in selection of colors, sizes of images, and sharpness of detail. An object in the foreground, for example, would have stronger color, sharper detail, and a larger size than an object farther away in the background. Surface texture must also be considered when painting trompe l'oeil effects, and many textures can be reproduced surprisingly well with artful application of paint.

Although gifted artists can often paint trompe l'oeil images freehand, I used the help of stencils to create the painted effects on Grandfather's desk. Shadow can be added by offsetting the stencil after the main image has been painted and adding a little gray or black paint to your color to create realistic shadow. I used water-based, acrylic paints and both stencil brushes and sea sponges to paint the desk, but I first practiced on cardboard to make sure I was getting the look I wanted and did a few pencil sketches on the desk before I applied paint. One trick in stenciling trompe l'oeil designs is to apply as little paint as possible at a time and add more paint as needed to achieve the desired effect. As a novice at trompe l'oeil, I also found it helpful to refer to art books obtained from my local public library as well as instructions included with the stencils.

I was delighted with the finished result on the desk, and it adds a unique touch to my newly redecorated study. Having never considered myself an artist, I was pleased to discover that I could create something so artistic. The highest praise, however, came from my mother when she saw the old desk transformed. She said that Grandfather would love it and would be quite pleased to see his neglected desk looking so beautiful in my home.

MINT

The Garden

Nancy Byrd Turner

Who rears four walls around a little plot—
Some still secluded spot—
And digs and sows therein has done a thing
Beyond his reckoning.
In one small, fended space,
Beauty and deep, untellable content
Make their abiding place,
And measureless peace is pent.
There time takes note of tender happenings:
The shimmer of a butterfly's blue wings
Above the clustered phlox;
A spider's will to work a miracle
Between two hollyhocks;
A twilight cricket's humble prophecies;
A brown bird by a pool; and all that goes
Into the lovely lifetime of a rose;
A pansy's lore; and little questing bees'
Strange, sweet biographies.

Who makes a garden, plans beyond his knowing.
Old roads are lost, old dwellings have their day,
And he himself, far summoned, passes hence
An unfamiliar way;
But lo, he has not perished with his going:
For year by year as April's heart is stirred,
Spring after punctual spring,
Across the little acre's wintry gray
Comes, slowly traced, an old, authentic word
In radiant lettering:
A shining script of tendril, vine, and whorl,
New green, faint rose, clear lavender, and pearl.
Petal by delicate petal, leaf by leaf,
As though his own hand from the mystery
Wrote for all earth to see,
Upon a fadeless beauteous scroll,
His brief, for immortality.

How could such sweet and wholesome hours
Be reckoned but with herbs and flowers? —Andrew Marvell

Some stone friends hide among the leaves in this herb garden in Fall City, Washington. Photo by Jessie Walker.

From My Garden Journal

Lisa Ragan

MOONFLOWER

My heart thrills on sunny spring mornings when I can devote two or three hours to my garden—digging, planting, kneeling, getting really close to the earth and smelling the richness there, smelling the spring season in the headiness of the soil. This morning found me repainting a wooden trellis and daydreaming of summer evenings to come, summer evenings that will find me relaxing on my favorite garden bench, sipping a tall glass of iced tea, and waiting. In my daydream, I can feel the lingering warmth of the last golden rays as the sun slowly slips beneath the horizon. Just across from the little garden bench, a moonflower vine climbs the wooden trellis, and my eyes focus on the many twisting buds the vine always has by mid-summer. Then, it happens. Slowly, ever so slowly, the moonflower's blossoms begin to open right before my eyes, unfurling the silky white petals into plate-sized blooms that reflect all the light of the shining moon. Sometimes the neighborhood children come by to witness the moonflower's nightly gift, and we delight together in this sprawling vine's magic. I breathe in deep to savor the moonflower's signature scent, but instead I am abruptly brought back to the present by the sharp smell of fresh paint on the brush in my hand. With a satisfied sigh, I finish putting the final coat of paint on the trellis and venture back in the house to check for sprouts in my small peat pots of moonflower seeds.

Native to the American tropics, the moonflower is a widely cultivated vine with night-blooming flowers that have a strong, sweet scent, a scent that has proven delightful to some and nearly suffocating to others. The vine is a close relative of the morning glory and the sweet potato vine and is sometimes called evening glory or moon vine. The official Latin name for moonflower is *Ipomoea alba*, although gardeners can sometimes still find it under its previous designation as *Calonyction aculeatum* in vintage gardening manuals and catalogs.

Moonflower vines thrive as lush perennials in their native tropical climates, including the warmer regions of the United States, but they can also be grown as annuals throughout most of the country. The vines themselves can climb from ten to thirty feet when well supported by a trellis or fence and feature large, heart-shaped leaves that can reach roughly eight inches in diameter. With its sprawling vines and twisting buds, the moonflower becomes almost sculptural

MOONFLOWER

as it grows. But it's for the blossoms, those heavenly blossoms, that gardeners cultivate this nighttime marvel.

As night descends, each bud gradually unfurls to reveal glossy white, paper-thin blooms that perfume the air with a saccharine-sweet, intoxicating aroma. The trumpet-shaped blossoms are reminiscent of the moonflower's cousin, the morning glory, but moonflower blossoms are significantly larger and bloom at the opposite end of the sundial. They will last throughout the night and on into the morning hours on overcast days before they succumb completely; alas, each blossom lasts but a single night. My theory argues that each blossom pours out so much energy in its beauty and scent that one night simply uses it all up. But never fear, more blossoms will appear by sundown the next evening. In fact, at the height of blooming season in mid-summer, the blooms will appear in such profusion as to nearly conceal the vine itself.

Although the moonflower is related to the morning glory, take care not to purchase the white cultivar of the morning glory, which is called *Ipomoea purpurea* "Alba." Gardeners may also find the moonflower under the names *Ipomoea grandiflora*, *Ipomoea noctiphiton*, *Ipomoea noctiflora*, and *Ipomoea bona-nox*; but *Ipomoea alba* is widely considered the standard moonflower. Moonflower blossoms are traditionally pure white, but some pale pink varieties are available.

Moonflower seeds can be sown directly in the ground in warm climates after all threat of frost has passed. Gardeners in northern climes can start their moonflower vines by planting seeds in peat pots in late April and placing them under grow lights or on a sunny, warm windowsill and then transplanting outdoors after the final frost. The seeds should be notched and then soaked in tepid water for about twenty-four hours before planting and will germinate in about seven to ten days. Select a sunny spot in your garden that has fertile, well-drained soil and retains moisture. If the vine receives at least six hours of full sun each day, it will use that soaked up energy for those spectacular blossoms at night. Once you've chosen the right spot for your garden, plant seeds or seedlings (depending on your climate) six to twelve inches apart and about one to two inches deep. Water daily until the vine becomes well-established. Propagation can be achieved with either cuttings or seeds. Some of the more old-fashioned gardeners subscribe to the belief that the most prolific moonflower vines grow when planted during the time of a new moon.

Usually a hardy vine, moonflower can sometimes be susceptible to canker, leaf spot, and rust. As for pests, the blossoms and leaves prove irresistible to deer in particular, so take heed if your garden is accessible to these night-grazing animals. Pets and children should be supervised when in contact with moonflower vines because they are toxic if ingested.

Now my sturdy trellis sports a fresh coat of paint, and my kitchen windowsill holds several little pots of germinating moonflower seeds, two of which have already delighted me with new green sprouts bursting through the soil—a visible reminder right here in my kitchen of the rebirth of spring, the resurrection of life. Soon the warming days will move beyond the last threat of frost, and I can transplant these little vines outdoors beneath the waiting trellis. My neighbors are quite used to the sight of me digging away in this patch or another in my garden, but I wonder what they'll think when they see me planting moonflower seedlings by the light of a shining new moon.

Lisa Ragan tends her small but mighty city garden in Nashville, Tennessee, with the help of her two shih-tzu puppies, Clover and Curry.

Seedtime

Philip Jerome Cleveland

Each year I plow the clover-scented loam,
Remembering, when sweet winds warm the glen,
That fields outlast the implements of man;
His furrow walls shall crumble soon again.
Each springtime, when I haul cordwood and logs,
I say that houses do not wear like hills
Where grizzled giants stand up to the stars
And wave their great arms when a passion wills!
The ferns, the clover, and the long sweet grass
I plow to make a bedding for my seed;
They spring eternal from the fresh, warm soil
To give man courage in his hour of need.

So while I plow the field and cart my wood,
Turn in the daisies and the sweet fern clod,
My face is to the furrow; but my heart
Leaps with the sudden meadowlark—to God.

In those vernal seasons of the year when the air is calm and pleasant, it were an injury and sullenness against nature not to go out and see her riches and partake in her rejoicing with heaven and earth.

— *John Milton*

A gambrel barn stands above an unplowed field in Colebrook, New Hampshire. Photo by William H. Johnson/Johnson's Photography.

Readers' Reflections

O Easter

Leah K. Nutter
Canton, Ohio

O Easter, did you drape the
Hills in lilies and daffodils,
And did you dress the trees
In pink and white
And cover the ground
In green so bright?
And O Easter, did you
Create a new birth
To celebrate new life
Upon this earth?
O Easter, did you
Paint the world in
So many pastels,
Completely unfurled?
And did you bring joy
To those around
And fill the air
With beautiful sound?

The Master's Garden

Hope C. Oberhelman
Lubbock, Texas

Help me cultivate Thy garden;
Help me plant it, row by row;
Keep me sowing, gracious Master,
That every seed may thrive and grow.

Help me cultivate Thy garden;
Help me plant each precious seed—
Hope and faith and love and mercy,
All the things my soul doth need.
Help me cultivate Thy garden;
Blessed Master, stay Thou near;
Help me water it and watch it
As each seedling doth appear.

Help me cultivate Thy garden;
Keep me sowing, O my Lord.
Help me labor in Thy garden,
Where every flower is a reward.

Springtime

Debra C. Williams
Hampton, Tennessee

Go outside on a beautiful spring morning
Just to enjoy the view.
Listen to the little birds singing;
See the tulips all covered with dew.

Notice all the trees that are budding,
The crocus peeping out of the ground.
The earth is full of fresh beauty;
Forsythia is blooming all around.

Baby birds are hatching in their nest
High up in the dogwood tree,
And if you listen very closely
You'll hear the buzz of a honeybee.

The earth has awakened
From a long winter's dream
And is bursting with beauty
Just waiting to be seen!

A Spring Parade

Nora M. Bozeman
Nixa, Missouri

A glorious day is unveiling;
A robin his song is regaling.
Sunbeams dance upon the dew
And sparkle spring in her debut.

The tulips are busily blooming;
The lilacs are sweetly perfuming.
The bumblebees and butterflies
Spread their wings 'neath azure skies.

A soft, gentle breeze is blowing;
A golden sunset is glowing.
As dusk pulls down her purple shade,
I marvel at God's spring parade.

Editor's Note: Readers are invited to submit original poetry for possible publication in future issues of Ideals. *Please send typed copies only; manuscripts will not be returned. Writers receive $10 for each published submission. Send material to Readers' Reflections, Ideals Publications, 535 Metroplex Drive, Suite 250, Nashville, Tennessee 37211.*

Spring Search

Myrtle George Latimer

We went in search, as princes, long ago,
To find a lady's-slipper. It must grow
In forests, where the humus, soft and brown,
Can nourish and sunlight gild its crown.

But more was found. My child is now aware
Of how the trees can speak. She can compare
Their whispers with a rushing river's peak,
Excitement in her voice and on her cheek.

A snail's home, dry hive of bees, the sweep
Of greening fields the heart can file and keep,
The quietness that brings to mind a song,
Brave thoughts that questing hearts can build upon.

We found our lady's-slipper—orchid rare,
And with it simple joy like silent prayer.

Golden lady's-slipper orchids reach toward the sun in Door County, Wisconsin. Photo by Darryl R. Beers.

Douglas Malloch

Art by Eve DeGrie

The Little Garden

Three rows of peas and three of beans,
Four hills, perhaps, of corn,
And maybe you don't think it means
So much, but every morn
They hurry out to see if night
Has brought another seed to light.

This row of radishes, the row
Of berry bushes too,
Have something more to make them grow
Than all your acres do.
They all have rain and sun above;
But these have more, for these have love.

The little gardens near the street,
Amid the city din,
Have always seemed to me the sweet,
The best to labor in,
When every tendril, every vine,
Around our happy hearts entwine.

For where love plants, there love will reap,
And reap a thousandfold;
And so a little garden keep
And watch its joy unfold.
With love to tend and turn the loam,
Who makes a garden makes a home.

Ideals' Family Recipes

Before the last chill leaves the air, take advantage of early spring's bounty of greens with these tasty dishes. We would love to try your favorite recipe too. Send a typed copy to Ideals Publications, 535 Metroplex Drive, Suite 250, Nashville, TN 37211. *We pay $10 for each recipe published.*

Spinach Casserole

Mrs. John B. Wright of Greenville, South Carolina

2 boxes frozen, chopped spinach
1 8-ounce package cream cheese, softened
½ cup butter, softened, divided
Zest of 1 small lemon
Juice of ½ lemon
Pinch nutmeg
1 cup dry dressing or stuffing mix

Preheat oven to 350° F. Cook spinach according to package directions; set aside. In a large bowl, combine cream cheese, ¼ cup of the butter, zest, juice, and nutmeg. Add hot spinach and mix well. Pour into a greased casserole dish. Top with dressing mix. Melt remaining ¼ cup butter and drizzle over top of casserole. Bake 30 minutes. Makes 6 to 8 servings.

Backwoods Spinach Salad

Jackie Kellogg of Grand Rapids, Michigan

½ cup uncooked wild rice
8 slices bacon, chopped
¼ cup apple cider vinegar
¼ teaspoon salt
¼ teaspoon pepper
2 tablespoons honey
4 cups torn spinach leaves
1 cup sliced mushrooms
1 cup sliced radishes

Cook wild rice according to package directions. Meanwhile, in large skillet, cook bacon over medium high heat until browned. Drain bacon, reserving 2 tablespoons grease. Set aside bacon and reserved grease. In same skillet, stir together vinegar, salt, pepper, honey, and reserved bacon grease. Cook over medium heat, stirring occasionally, until heated through (3 to 4 minutes). In a large bowl, combine rice and bacon with spinach, mushrooms, and radishes. Pour warm dressing over salad; toss and serve immediately. Makes 6 servings.

Endive and Apple Salad

Rose Bucks of Boyertown, Pennsylvania

- 5 tablespoons vegetable oil
- 2 teaspoons cider vinegar
- 4 teaspoons water
- ¼ teaspoon salt
- ¼ teaspoon pepper
- 1 teaspoon granulated sugar
- 1 medium bunch endive
- 2 apples, peeled and sliced

In a small bowl, combine first 6 ingredients. Set aside. Cut endive into strips. In a medium bowl, combine the endive and apples; toss. Pour vinegar mixture over the salad. Toss and serve immediately. Makes 6 servings.

Scalloped Cabbage

Betsy A. Campbell of Springtown, Texas

- 1 medium head green cabbage, chopped
- 1 medium onion, diced
- ½ cup water
- 5 tablespoons butter, divided
- 2 tablespoons all-purpose flour
- 1 cup milk
- 1 teaspoon salt
- ¾ cup shredded Cheddar cheese
- ¼ cup bread crumbs

Preheat oven to 350° F. In a large saucepan, place chopped cabbage, onion, and water. Cover and steam until tender; drain. Spoon into greased baking dish; set aside. In a small saucepan over low heat, melt 3 tablespoons of the butter. Stir in flour until smooth. Add milk, stirring constantly, until smooth. Add salt and cheese, stirring until cheese is melted. Pour cheese mixture over cabbage mixture. Sprinkle with bread crumbs, then dot with remaining butter. Bake 30 minutes or until golden brown. Makes 6 servings.

Tangy Kale

Estella Wiens of Willow Street, Pennsylvania

- 1 large bunch kale
- 2 tablespoons vegetable oil
- 1 clove garlic, minced
- ½ cup water
- 1 tablespoon apple cider vinegar
- Salt to taste

Remove ribs from kale. Chop leaves; set aside. In a large skillet, heat oil and garlic. Add kale and sauté 5 minutes. Add water; cover and steam 5 minutes. Drain. Sprinkle with vinegar; salt to taste. Mix and serve immediately. Makes 6 servings.

Jeweled Spring Morn

Mildred L. Jarrell

Early morning sunbeams
Sparkle on the dew,
Twinkle on a spider web
Silvery and new.

Flashing on the meadow pond,
Winking through the trees,
Radiance rims the water wheel
Glistening o'er the stream.

Crystal beads the tulip cups,
Dew diamonds tip the grass,
Magic of a jeweled morn,
Oh, that it could last.

A spider web glistens with its early morning jewels.
Photo by H. Richard Johnston/FPG International.

Spring Morning

Mona K. Guldswog

I awake in the morning and am keenly aware
Of the trill of birds,
The scent of lily of the valley
Lovingly planted 'neath our bedroom window,
And the bright, clean freshness of rain-washed air.

Fresh Outlook

D. A. Hoover

As strawberry rays of sunrise
Brush away cobwebs of dark,
Silver veils of mist are draping
Gossamer above the park.

There's a fresh new diamond sparkle
Of small jewels on the lawn
And a reborn zest for living
Coming to us every dawn.

Bits and Pieces

Some people are like ants. Give them a warm day and a piece of ground and they start digging.

—Hal Borland

They who labor in the earth are the chosen people of God.

—Thomas Jefferson

To own a bit of ground, to scratch it with a hoe, to plant seeds and watch the renewal of life, this is the commonest delight of the race, the most satisfactory thing a man can do.

—Charles Dudley Warner

All through the long winter I dream of my garden. On the first warm day of spring I dig my fingers deep into the soft earth. I can feel its energy, and my spirits soar.

—Helen Hayes

In March and in April from morning till night
In sowing and seeding good housewives delight.

—Thomas Tusser

I do not know what you have been doing this morning; for my part, I have been in the dew up to my knees, laying lindens.

—*Madame de Sevigné*

*T*here can be no other occupation like gardening in which, if you were to creep up behind someone at their work, you would find them smiling.

—*Mirabel Osler*

*T*o a certain extent we raise a garden as we might a child, putting in the seed, nourishing it and gathering nourishment from it, pruning and weeding its growth, protecting it, loving it, worrying over it.

—*Robert Finch*

*H*ow can one help shivering with delight when one's hot fingers close around the stem of a live flower, cool from the shade and stiff with newborn vigor?

—*Colette*

Opportunity

Louise Weibert Sutton

Now birds, all colors, soaring 'round,
Skim trails of golden air
As apple blossoms, petalled pink,
Meet snowy, scented pear;
And purple-carpeted, the grass
With violets now lies
Beneath the sheer, blue magic of
Spring's cloud-capped morning skies!
Too rarely comes, too swiftly goes
Gay April, warm and fair,
While May herself can hardly wait
To follow down the stair.
No other season holds such blend
Of earth and heaven in it,
And I intend to make the most
Of every lovely minute!

A Breath of Spring

Nora M. Bozeman

April bathes in the breath of spring
And borrows a robin's song to sing.
She lilac-lines the lanes with care
And scatters tulips everywhere.

April emeralds fields and hills
And golds the garden with daffodils.
She wears a glistened dewdrop gown
With white-washed daisies for her crown.

April bathes in the breath of spring,
Awakens every living thing;
Then fancy-free she wends her way
Into the merry month of May.

Stone steps wind through a mossy hillside at Washington Park in Portland, Oregon. Photo by Terry Donnelly.

Readers' Forum

Snapshots from Our Ideals *Readers*

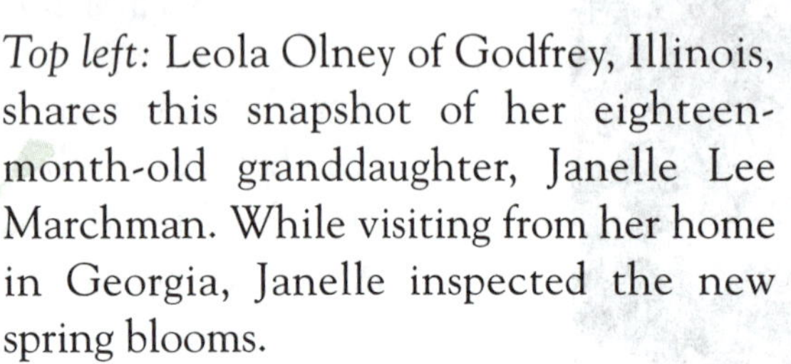

Top left: Leola Olney of Godfrey, Illinois, shares this snapshot of her eighteen-month-old granddaughter, Janelle Lee Marchman. While visiting from her home in Georgia, Janelle inspected the new spring blooms.

Top right: Who could be upset with this face, even if little Trevor Tuman was caught crawling out of the middle of the flowers in his mother's rock garden? This snapshot was sent to us by Trevor's grandmother, Jeanne Tuman of Hutchinson, Minnesota.

Lower right: Chloe Rita Taylor, age three, is ready for the next spring shower. Chloe, who lives in Louisiana, always enjoys visiting her Grandma and Grandpa, Z. L. and Bettye Taylor, in Pittsburg, Texas.

Top left: Marcia Hancock of Shoreline, Washington, shares this photo of her grandchildren amid a sea of red tulips. Proud Grandma Marcia could argue that even the flowers' beauty can't upstage Linsey (age four years), Lara (age five years), and Landon (age two years) Curry.

Middle left: What could be sweeter than one little girl in her Easter finery? Twins! PaPa and Grandma Frick of West Seneca, New York, say that two-and-a-half-year-old Andee Elizabeth and Jaycee Jule bring happiness and love to everyone they meet.

Lower left: One year old Rae Garner can't help crying when she doesn't uncover as many Easter eggs as big brother Todd, age three. Rae and Todd are the great-grandchildren of Clara Taylor (known as "Mimi" to the kids) of Wynne, Arkansas.

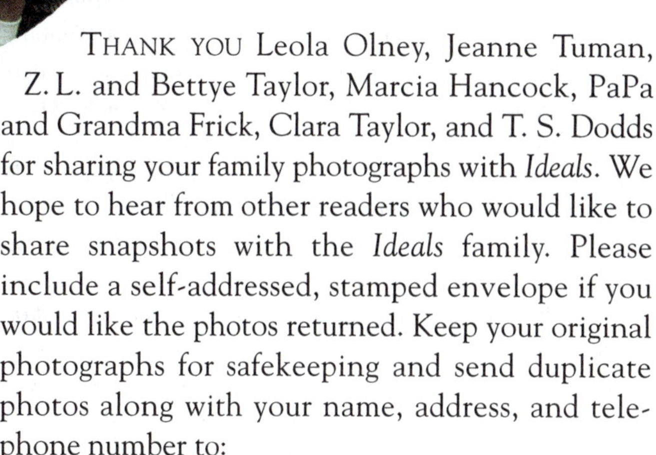

THANK YOU Leola Olney, Jeanne Tuman, Z. L. and Bettye Taylor, Marcia Hancock, PaPa and Grandma Frick, Clara Taylor, and T. S. Dodds for sharing your family photographs with *Ideals*. We hope to hear from other readers who would like to share snapshots with the *Ideals* family. Please include a self-addressed, stamped envelope if you would like the photos returned. Keep your original photographs for safekeeping and send duplicate photos along with your name, address, and telephone number to:

Readers' Forum
Ideals Publications
535 Metroplex Drive, Suite 250
Nashville, Tennessee 37211

T. S. Dodds of Florida shares this photograph of daughter Lian Dodds, who is contemplating a flower fairy. Sweet Lian is twenty-three months old.

ideals®

Publisher, Patricia A. Pingry
Editor, Michelle Prater Burke
Designer, Marisa Calvin
Managing Editor, Peggy Schaefer
Copy Editor, Amy Johnson
Editorial Assistant, Patsy Jay
Contributing Editors, Lansing Christman, Pamela Kennedy, Nancy Skarmeas, and Lisa Ragan
Production Manager, Travis Rader

Acknowledgments

COATSWORTH, ELIZABETH. "The Sun Comes Dancing." Reprinted by permission of Catherine Beston Barnes. HOLMES, MARJORIE. "The Easter Eggs" from *Love and Laughter.* Copyright © 1967 by Marjorie Holmes. Used by permission of the author. RICH, LOUISE DICKINSON. Excerpts from "How Firm a Foundation" from *Innocence Under the Elms.* Copyright © 1955 by Louise Dickinson Rich. Used by permission of Curtis Brown, Ltd. STEVENS, RUTH W. "Easter Prayer" from *Christian Home,* Vol. 24, No. 8, April 1965. Copyright © 1965 by Graded Press. Used by permission of Abingdon Press. Our sincere thanks to the following authors whom we were unable to locate: Louise Abney for "Easter Morning"; Philip Jerome Cleveland for "Seedtime"; Merle Marquis Frank for "Easter Joy"; Methyl Hawkins for "The Road to Emmaus"; Brian F. King for "Awakening"; Jane Merchant for "Jonquil Lore" from *Halfway Up the Sky;* and Ernest Boyle O'Reilly for "Easter Morn."

STATEMENT OF OWNERSHIP, MANAGEMENT, AND CIRCULATION (REQUIRED BY FORM 3526)

1. Publication Title: Ideals. 2. Publication Number: 0019-137X. 3. Filing Date: August 24, 2001. 4. Issue Frequency: 6. 5. Number of Issues Published Annually: 6. 6. Annual Subscription Price: $19.95. 7. Office of publication: Guideposts, A Church Corporation, 39 Seminary Hill Road, Carmel, NY 10512. 8. Location of headquarters: Guideposts, A Church Corporation, 39 Seminary Hill Road, Carmel, NY 10512. 9. The names and addresses of the publisher and the editor-in-chief are: Patricia A. Pingry, Ideals Publications, A Division of Guideposts, 535 Metroplex Dr., Ste. 250, Nashville, TN 37211; Editor: Michelle Prater Burke (same as publisher); Managing Editor: Michelle Prater Burke (same as publisher). 10. Owner: Guideposts, A Church Corporation, a New York not for-profit corporation, 39 Seminary Hill Road, Carmel, NY 10512. Names and addresses of individual owners: None. 11. The known bondholders, mortgagees, and other security holders owning or holding one percent or more of total amount of bonds, mortgages or other securities: None. 12. The exempt status has not changed during preceding 12 months. 13. Publication Name: Ideals. 14. Issue Date for Circulation Data: Thanksgiving '00 thru Friendship '01. 15. Average number of copies each issue during preceding twelve months: a. total number of copies printed: 225,316; b. (1) paid and/or requested circulation through outside-county mail subscriptions: 170,495; (2) paid and/or requested circulation through in-county subscriptions: None; (3) paid and/or requested circulation through dealer sales: 26,355; (4) paid and/or requested circulation through other classes: None; c. total paid and/or requested circulation: 196,850. d. (1) free distribution by mail through outside-county: 845; (2) free distribution by mail through in-county: None; (3) free distribution by mail through other classes: None; e. free distribution outside the mail: None; f. total free distribution: 845; g. total distribution: 197,695; h. copies not distributed: 27,621; i. total: 225,316. Percent Paid and/or requested circulation: 99.6%. 15. Actual number of copies of single issue published nearest to filing date: a. total number of copies printed: 169,589; b. (1) paid and/or requested circulation through outside-county mail subscriptions: 150,460; (2) paid and/or requested circulation through in-county subscriptions: None; (3) paid and/or requested circulation through dealer sales: 7,424; (4) paid and/or requested circulation through other classes: None; c. total paid and/or requested circulation: 157,884; d. (1) free distribution by mail through outside-county: 774; (2) free distribution by mail through in-county: None; (3) free distribution by mail through other classes: None; e. free distribution outside the mail: None; f. total free distribution: 774; g. total distribution: 158,658; h. copies not distributed: 10,931; i. total: 169,589. Percent Paid and/or requested circulation: 99.5%. 16. This Statement of Ownership will be printed in the Easter '02 issue of this publication. 17. I certify that the statements made to me above are correct and complete. Signed John F. Temple, President.